SEASON OF PROMISES

Praying through Advent with

Julian of Norwich
Thomas à Kempis
Caryll Houselander
Thomas Merton
Brother Lawrence
Max Picard

MITCH FINLEY

D1125686

Resurrection Press
Mineola • New York

Other books by Mitch Finley:

Building Christian Families (with Kathy Finley; Thomas More Press).

Catholic Spiritual Classics (Sheed & Ward)

Time Capsules of the Church (Our Sunday Visitor Books)

Your Family in Focus: Appreciating What You Have, Making It Even Better (Ave Maria Press)

Everybody Has a Guardian Angel . . . And Other Lasting Lessons I Learned in Catholic Schools (Crossroad Publishing Co.)

Heavenly Helpers: St. Anthony and St. Jude (Crossroad Publishing Co.)

Catholic Is Wonderful (Resurrection Press)

Whispers of Love: Inspiring Encounters with Deceased Relatives and Friends (Crossroad Publishing Co.)

First published in 1995 by Resurrection Press, Ltd.
P.O. Box 248
Williston Park, NY 11596

ISBN 1-878718-31-2

Cover design by John Murello

Printed in the United States of America.

Introduction

Advent is a lonely step-child of a season; it does not get the respect it deserves. Too often Advent gets lost in our wild dash toward Christmas. But look. Advent is the season of promises, filled with spiritual riches for those ready to accept its blessings. Advent is a season of promises.

In his song, "The Boxer," singer-song writer Paul Simon croons about "a pocket full of mumbles, such are promises." But not in this case. Advent is loaded with promises for a future we already have. It's a mystical season, full of promises already kept, promises from God to be Emmanuel, "God with us," always. Always. No pocket full of mumbles here. Only promises fulfilled, promises kept.

Only if we dive deeply into Advent will Christmas deliver its deepest blessings, however. Only if we dive deeply. No need to take hours a day to do this, of course. A few minutes each day will do ya. Just a few minutes to consciously open oneself to the true spirit of Advent, the promises of Advent.

This collection of Advent reflections is unique. Most daily reflections take their cue from scripture, which is excellent. This little book takes a unique approach, relying on inspiration from a different source, six classics of spiritual literature — three modern, three many centuries old. This has the advantage of variety and means the reader need not be chained to the liturgical readings being used this year. At least not for these meditations.

The classics I draw from are: *The World of Silence*, by Max Picard (1952), *The Reed of God*, by Caryll Houselander (1944), *New Seeds of Contemplation,* by Thomas Merton (1961), *The Imitation of Christ,* by Thomas à Kempis (15th century), *Revelations of Divine Love,* by Julian of Norwich (14th century), and *The Practice of the Presence of God,* by Brother Lawrence (17th century).

For each day of Advent — and there are enough meditations here to cover the longest possible Advent — you will find a brief excerpt from one of these spiritual classics, followed by a reflection by the author and a one-sentence prayer. It's as simple as that. No profound method of prayer here. Follow the quotations, the meditation, and/or the little prayer for each day wherever they may lead you. It's as simple as that.

One last thing: May your Advent season be filled with blessings undreamed of and lead you to a special Christmas, indeed.

First Sunday of Advent

"I turn my little omelette in the pan for the love of God. When it is finished, if I have nothing to do, I prostrate myself on the ground and worship my God, who gave me the grace to make it, after which I arise happier than a king. When I can do nothing else, it is enough to have picked up a straw for the love of God."

— BROTHER LAWRENCE,
The Practice of the Presence of God

ADVENT GRACES THE WEEKS before Christmas, but if we're not careful it gets lost in the holiday shuffle. We all do the holiday shuffle. The weeks before Christmas can be hectic, so full of pre-Christmas activities that we miss its true spirit, which is a spirit of holiness in the midst of the ordinary.

What is Christmas but the celebration of God's love for the ordinary? When the Son of God is born he does not come in a spectacular manner, and the first to get the news is a crew of bumpkin shepherds. Jesus is born in the most ordinary circumstances, and he comes into the world in the usual way — "born of a woman," St. Paul reminds us (Gal 4:4). So Advent is a time to remember the holiness of the ordinary.

The ordinary world and ordinary life are so good that God's own Son embraced it for himself. Look around at all the ordinariness in your life. There you are, and it's all holy because God is present in ordinary situations.

Look. Look closely. Look quietly. Look prayerfully. The smallest, most ordinary task is holy. Brother Lawrence, a nobody cook in an obscure 17th-century French monastery, turned a little omelette in a pan and saw that it was holy. He picked up a straw from the floor and saw that this was holy. All the ordinary things in your life are holy, too.

God of the ordinary, help me during Advent
to be more prayerfully aware of your presence
in the ordinary activities
of my ordinary day. Amen.

First Monday of Advent

"If you have money, consider that perhaps the only reason God allowed it to fall into your hands was in order that you might find joy and perfection by giving it all away."

— THOMAS MERTON, New Seeds of Contemplation

SOMETIMES IT IS EASY for Advent to get mixed up with the great American season of shopping. We call it the "Shopping Season," even capitalizing the first letters of the words. Heavy duty stuff, here. The Shopping Season!

Peculiar things go on in our heads during the Christmas Shopping Season. We get discombobulated. In our heart, and in our mind, we get discombobulated. We get the Shopping Season mixed up with the most remarkable things. Love, for example. We get Shopping mixed up with love. We honestly think that if we truly love someone we must Go Shopping and buy that person a Gift. Otherwise, he or she will not feel loved. Trouble is, often the people we feel we must buy Gifts for do, in fact, feel that way. If we don't buy them Gifts, they will feel unloved.

'Tis a puzzlement, as the king says in the musical, *The King and I*. Indeed it is. What a strange world we live in, where love and feeling loved require the giving of Gifts, and not just any gifts, mind you. Especially when it comes to children, we must buy them the Latest Things, the Current Craze, otherwise they will feel unloved. We believe that we are bad parents and grandparents if we don't buy the children What They Want.

Maybe it can't be helped. Not entirely, at least. But we can do something. We can modify perceptions. We can make a big deal out of giving away money to worthy causes for Christmas, too. We can make sure the children see us doing as much for those who have nothing as we do for those who have plenty. During Advent we can do this. We can.

God of Advent, fill my heart with a deep desire to show love for those who have little. Amen.

First Tuesday of Advent

"[God] is our clothing. In his love he wraps and holds us. He enfolds us for love, and he will never let us go...I saw that he is to us everything that is good."

— Julian of Norwich, Revelations of Divine Love

THE ADVENT SEASON is a season of homely things — "homely" in the dictionary's first meaning of the word, "characteristic of the home or of home life." Advent is a season of homely things because during this season we prepare for the coming of a homely God, a God who is at home with us. Our God is so at home with us that Dame Julian of Norwich, a 13th-century homely English mystic and all-around practical person, said that God is "our clothing." Imagine that.

Here we go through our day with God as our clothing, head to toe. God is our underwear. God is our socks and shoes. God is our dress or skirt, or God is our pants and shirt. If we live where winters are cold, God is the coat we put on before we go outside to face the cold. God is the muffler we wrap around our neck, and God is the winter hat we put upon our head. Imagine that.

Here we go during Advent, and God is our clothing. Looking forward to the birth of the Messiah, and God is our clothing. Oh delightful idea. Oh marvelous thing to recall while dressing in the morning. At night, when we prepare for sleep, God is the pajamas or nightgown we put on before we slip beneath the covers. Imagine that.

If we think of God as our clothing we will have less anxiety about "measuring up" to the standards established by a commercially driven fashion industry. If God is our clothing, during Advent we can think more about "putting on the Lord Jesus Christ" (see Rom 13:14). Imagine that.

Lord our God, help me to trust more
in your constant love that surrounds me
and all those I love. Amen.

First Wednesday of Advent

"[Silence] makes things whole again, by taking them back from the world of dissipation into the world of wholeness. It gives things something of its own holy uselessness, for that is what silence itself is: holy uselessness."

— MAX PICARD, The World of Silence

ADVENT IS A QUIET TIME. But Advent is sometimes overwhelmed by the noise and activity of the Shopping Season. What can we do? What? We can carve out a few minutes each day — at the beginning of the day, perhaps, or at the end of the day — when nothing happens except waiting in silence for the coming of Christ. Nothing except waiting in silence, holy silence.

In the first decade of the 20th century, a young Swiss physician, Max Picard, grew disillusioned with a medical profession that was losing sight of the humanity of the patient. Max Picard left medicine, moved to an obscure little village, and became a Catholic philosopher. He wrote about silence and the holy uselessness of silence.

The first Advent was a time of silence when all the world was at peace. The shepherds watched in silence. The magi, atop their loping camels, rode in silence across the silent desert. The animals in the stable waited in silence.... During this Advent, then, should we not spend a little time each day waiting in holy silence for the coming of Christ at Christmas? Should we not take time every day to set aside the activities of the Shopping Season so we can wait in the holy uselessness of silence?

If we wonder how Advent can come alive, have more meaning for us as a religious season, this is how. This is how. If we wait in holy silence for a few minutes each day of Advent, then this holy season will come alive. If we do nothing but wait and hope. In silence.

Lord of Advent, help me to await your coming in holy silence. Amen.

First Thursday of Advent

"Strangely enough, those who complain the loudest of the emptiness of their lives are usually people whose lives are overcrowded, filled with trivial details, plans, desires, ambitions.... Those who complain in these circumstances of the emptiness of their lives are usually afraid to allow space or silence or pause in their lives."

— CARYLL HOUSELANDER, The Reed of God

Quiet NOW. Pause. Attend. Advent is a time to cultivate the sheerest, most blissful emptiness. Advent is a time to cultivate — metaphorically speaking — the emptiness of the waiting womb, the womb waiting to receive and give birth to the Son of God. Quiet now. Pause. Attend.

During the Shopping Season, our lives fit the description offered by Caryll Houselander, a mid-20th-century English Catholic sculptor, writer, odd duck, party-goer, and lover of life. During the Shopping Season our lives often are filled with activity: "trivial details, plans, desires, ambitions." But in the random quiet moment, if we allow ourselves to reflect, we feel empty, the emptiness of a life void of meaning and purpose.

The only way to fill the emptiness that has no meaning is to cultivate the emptiness that does have meaning, the emptiness of the waiting womb. We cultivate this rich, nourishing Advent emptiness when we take a few minutes each day for *nothing.* We cultivate this warm Advent emptiness when we make time each day to wait for the sake of waiting, to hope for the sake of hoping, to be empty for the sake of being empty. We nourish Advent emptiness in ourselves when we make some space in each day to do nothing but open our heart to the coming of Christ. Quiet now. Pause. Attend.

Lord Jesus, help me to be open to your coming,
to wait, to be empty for you alone
to fill my heart. Amen.

First Friday of Advent

"Whoever follows me will never walk in darkness but will have the light of life" [Jn 8: 12b], *says the Lord.*

"By these words, Christ urges us to mold our lives and characters in the image of his, if we wish to be truly enlightened and freed from all blindness of heart. Let us therefore see that we endeavor beyond all else to meditate on the life of Jesus Christ."

— THOMAS À KEMPIS, The Imitation of Christ

W E THINK OF "meditation" as esoteric, the concern of folks who live in monasteries, of interest to the occasional odd duck. The wandering guru from India teaches "meditation." Certainly, we think, meditation is not to be taken seriously by your average person with a real life to live, mortgage or rent payments to make, a job to hold down, children to raise, a spouse to be married to and a car that needs an oil change.

Here's the thing. We meditate every time we turn around. At its most basic, to meditate merely means "to reflect upon or ponder." Without thinking, we meditate upon the values, ideals, and goals cherished by "the world." We reflect upon how much we would like to have a great pile of money, then we buy a lottery ticket. We ponder the satisfaction to be had from owning a new car, if only we had the money to buy one. . . .

When Thomas à Kempis wrote *The Imitation of Christ* in the early 15th century, he understood human nature well. He knew the need we have to meditate upon the Gospels if we are to be "truly enlightened and freed from all blindness of heart." This meditation is no esoteric matter. All we need do is take a few minutes each day to reflect upon a few lines from the Gospels.

God of love, during Advent help me to have the desire to read and reflect upon the Gospels, that I might be freed from all blindness of heart. Amen.

First Saturday of Advent

"[God] does not ask much of us — an occasional remembrance, a small act of worship, now to beg his grace, at times to offer him our distresses, at another time to render thanks for the favors he has given, and which he gives in the midst of your labors. ...At table and in the midst of conversation, lift your heart at times towards him. It is not needful at such times to cry out loud. He is nearer to us than we think."

— BROTHER LAWRENCE,
The Practice of the Presence of God

ADVENT IS A QUIET SEASON. Quiet. Listen. Advent whispers, and we must be quiet if we are to hear its message. Advent whispers. Listen carefully. Advent carries a quiet message, it says that God is near, our God is near, our God who is unlimited, unconditional love, is near.

Can we believe this? Advent calls to us in whispers. Remember that God is love, and remember that God is near. That is the message of the Incarnation, the message of Advent, the message of Christmas, that God is nearer to us than we can begin to imagine. Imagine it all the same. God is near. Advent whispers a message of infinite compassion and love, compassion and love, and we find it difficult to believe.

Oh, we are ready to believe it on a theoretical level. God is love, and God is nearer to us than we think. But are we ready to believe it on the level of the heart? We must, if the message is to transform our lives. Advent whispers the message, but not in our ears. No. Advent whispers the message, whispers the message, but in our heart. That is where we must hear it, in our heart. We must listen not with our ears but with our heart. Advent whispers that God is nearer to us than we think, and that is the message of the Christmas we look forward to, that God is so near to us, so near.

We need not cry out loud for God to hear us, for God is nearer to us than we think. All we need do is whisper. Whisper silently in the quiet of our heart. God is so near.

Loving God, help me to remember how near you are, and help me to call upon you often in the silence of my heart. Amen.

Second Sunday of Advent

"Every one of us forms an idea of Christ that is limited and incomplete. It is cut according to our own measure. We tend to create for ourselves a Christ in our own image, a projection of our own aspirations, desires and ideals. We find in Him what we want to find. We make Him not only the incarnation of God but also the incarnation of the things we and our society and our part of society happen to live for."

— Thomas Merton, New Seeds of Contemplation

WHO IS THE JESUS you look forward to during Advent? What does he look like? Your description reveals more than you think. If you describe Jesus one way, remember that your description does not rule out other acceptable descriptions. Does your Jesus have the skin color and features characteristic of people who live today in the part of the world where Jesus lived nearly 2,000 years ago? Or do you carry in your head an image of Jesus from an artistic portrayal? The possibilities are almost endless.

During Advent, do you look forward to Baby Jesus, meek and mild? Or do you probe the Gospel accounts of Jesus' birth, prodding them to give up their teachings about the character of a faith for adult believers who live in the real world? During Advent, do you ask why the stories include shepherds, and an inn with no rooms available, and magi, and all the rest? Are these simply charming elements of the charming stories about the birth of Jesus in Bethlehem? Or is there more?

What does the Christ you hope for during Advent stand for? What ideals does he represent? Is he a Christ who offers comfort only, or does he challenge you as well? Does he come at Christmas leaving behind only the status quo? Or does he leave you unsettled, vulnerable, out in the open?

Lord Jesus, during Advent help me to deepen my idea of who you are and what you stand for. Amen.

Second Monday of Advent

"I set my heart on God with all my trust and with all my might . . . He wills that our hearts should be lifted high above the depths of earthly and vain sorrows, and rejoice in him . . . He loves us and enjoys us, and so he wills that we love him and enjoy him, and firmly trust him; and all shall be well."

— JULIAN OF NORWICH, Revelations of Divine Love

ADVENT HAS ONE MESSAGE that is rock bottom. The rock bottom message of Advent is a message of hope. Hope is not in vain, the spirit of Advent sings to us. If we listen. The heart of Advent is hope, and the spirit of Advent sings in our heart. If we listen. Hope, hope. Look forward to the birth of Christ with hope because no hope is more reliable. No matter what sorrows we have, they are small potatoes compared to the hope we have, the hope that is the heart of Advent.

No matter what sorrows we have, they are passing sorrows, in the long run, to be forgotten in the light of a joy that will have no end because it had no beginning because it is a joy that is eternal. No matter what sorrows we have, no matter how deep they are, the spirit of Advent sings, they are passing sorrows. This, too, shall pass. Our sorrows are real, they are not an illusion, but they are passing sorrows.

The final, bottom line, ultimate truth — the spirit of Advent sings — is this: God enjoys us and we are created to enjoy God. This is it! This is why the Son of God became a human being, because God enjoys us so much that to become one of us was too much to pass up. God enjoys us, and we are to enjoy God, and that is the heart of the joy we are created for. Imagine that.

The spirit of Advent sings that our sorrows are passing, there is hope, and we are meant to have a mutual enjoyment society with God. This, oh this, is what Christmas is supposed to remind us about. There can be no greater joy.

Lord of Advent, help me to keep my sorrows
at arm's length, and help me to enjoy you
and take joy knowing that you enjoy me. Amen.

Second Tuesday of Advent

"The nearness of silence means also the nearness of forgiveness and the nearness of love, for the natural basis of forgiveness and of love is silence. It is important that this natural basis should be there, for it means that forgiveness and love do not have first to create the medium in which they appear."

— MAX PICARD, The World of Silence

W HERE ARE YOU right now, this minute, as you read these words? Where are you? Where are you not only physically — in a house or apartment, in a church, riding on a train, bus, airplane or subway — but where are you in your heart and in your mind? In your mind, are you in a quiet place or a noisy place? Is your heart quiet or full of noise?

To wait quietly during Advent is to make ready a place for the birth of Christ to happen. To wait quietly during Advent is to prepare a place for love and forgiveness to appear in our heart. To prepare a quiet place is to prepare a place to be filled by the joy of Christmas. If we do not empty a place there will be no place. If we do not have a quiet place there will be no place, and the love and forgiveness that are the gifts of Christmas will find no place in us.

Apart from an appreciation for silence — real silence, silence of the heart — we have but an incomplete grasp of Advent. Advent waits quietly for the fullness of God's forgiveness and love to come into the world at Christmas. Advent waits quietly, and if we wait quietly, too, open to the true spirit of Advent, then we will experience the true spirit of Advent.

How to nourish a quiet heart in a noisy world? It's perfectly possible. If we want some quiet in our life each day we will make some quiet in our life each day. We will. It's as simple as that. And if we don't, we won't. It's as simple as that.

Loving God of Advent, help me to make
a time for quiet each day during Advent,
so there will be a quiet place for love
and forgiveness to enter in. Amen.

Second Wednesday of Advent

"Sometimes it may seem to us that there is no purpose in our lives, that going day after day for years to this office or that school or factory is nothing else but waste and weariness. But it may be that God has sent us there because but for us Christ would not be there. If our being there means that Christ is there, that alone makes it worth while."

— Caryll Houselander, The Reed of God

ET THE QUIET SPIRIT of Advent soak into your heart. Let the spirit of waiting patiently for the coming of Christ at Christmas soak into your heart. Now listen. Listen. The spirit of Advent is the spirit of the gospel, plain and simple. To open our heart to the true spirit of Advent is to open our heart to the gospel, the Good News that invites us to a new way of thinking and a new way of living. Plain and simple.

Shed your old way of thinking and living, the gospel says. Let your heart shed its old ways and leave them behind. Embrace a new way. Embrace a new way of thinking and living, a new way of seeing and hearing, a new way, a new way. No longer see as the world would have you see. Instead, see with the eyes of faith, of loving trust in God's love for you. See with the eyes of faith, of loving trust that God is in your life transforming, redeeming, bringing you to new birth.

See with the eyes of Advent. See that you are sent to bring the Spirit of Christ into your family, into your place of work — no matter how much you may or may not like your work. You are sent to bring the quiet spirit of Advent, the spirit of love, forgiveness, compassion, and peace. You are sent to bring the spirit of justice which is not hard as nails but strong, resilient, understanding, and determined.

Lord Jesus, during Advent help me to seek and find you in my place of work, and help me to bring you there in my heart. Amen.

Second Thursday of Advent

"The person who cares nothing for praise or blame knows great inward peace, and it is easy for the person whose conscience is clean to find contentment and quiet. Praise does not make you holier than you are, nor blame more wicked. You are exactly what you are — you cannot be said to be any better than you are in the eyes of God."

— Thomas à Kempis, The Imitation of Christ

ADVENT IS A TIME to cultivate genuine humility. Be only what you are, no more, no less. Take Mary as the model of humility. When the angel says, guess what, you're going to be the mother of the Messiah, what does Mary say? "Oh gosh, I'm way too unworthy, you'd better find somebody else"? No. Mary says, "Let it be with me according to your word" (Lk 1:48). Who is she to question God's judgement? Who is she to blow against the wind?

Who are we to question God's judgement? Echoing the cartoon character, Popeye, we can say, "I yam what I yam, and that's all what I yam." God calls us just as we are to be all that we can be. Who are we to blow against the wind?

Later, when Mary visits her cousin Elizabeth, and Elizabeth waxes on at some length in praise of what God is doing through Mary, does Mary go into a fit of false humility? "Oh gosh, please, it's no big deal." No. She does not question Elizabeth's evaluation of the situation. Instead, she joins Elizabeth in praising God who is the only one to whom praise is due anyway. "My soul magnifies the Lord, and my spirit rejoices in God my Savior, for he has looked with favor on the lowliness of his servant. Surely, from now on all generations will call me blessed..." (Lk 1:46–48).

The spirit of Advent whispers: Be all you are called to be, like Mary, and give thanks to God, like Mary.

Lord of Advent, help me to be all
that you call me to be, and help my heart
to be filled with prayerful praise
and thanksgiving to you. Amen.

Second Friday of Advent

"My commonest attitude is this simple attentiveness, an habitual, loving turning of my eyes to God, to whom I often find myself bound with more happiness and gratification than that which a babe enjoys clinging to its nurse's breast. So, if I dare use this expression, I should be glad to describe this condition as "the breasts of God," for the inexpressible happiness I savor and experience there."

— Brother Lawrence,
The Practice of the Presence of God

I N ADVENT, we look forward to commemorating the arrival on this earth of the Son of God as a helpless infant. Look. Take the infancy of the Son of God seriously. Here is God, present in a tiny newborn baby. How can this be? We take it for granted. Oh, well. Ho hum. You know. God is in this baby. Oh, well. Ho hum.

But look. Is this not absurd? The very idea. The Creator of the Universe, the Ground of All Being, the Great Cosmic Wherewithal, God, is in this little baby? The very idea. But this is what we believe. This. Nothing else. So what can we learn from this belief? Much. Endlessly. But include this in what we can learn, that God's love knows no limits. So great is God's love for us that no dimension of human existence, except sin, is off limits to God. Even nine months in the womb. Even death.

We may ask: How do we feel about God? We have ideas about God, but what are our feelings toward God? It is good for everyone, not just mystics, to have feelings of love for God, to desire God, to crave union with God. How often do we open ourselves to such feelings for God? Advent is a time to long passionately for God. Advent is a time to want to hold God in our arms like a tiny infant, or turn to God as a baby turns for sweet nourishment to its mother's breasts. Advent is such a time. It is.

God of Advent joy, fill my heart with a loving
desire for union with you, and help me
to turn to you with all my hopes,
anxieties, fears and joys. Amen.

Second Saturday of Advent

"Place no hope in the feeling of assurance, in spiritual comfort. You may well have to get along without this. Place no hope in the inspirational preachers of Christian sunshine, who are able to pick you up and set you back on your feet and make you feel good for three or four days — until you fold up and collapse into despair."

— Thomas Merton, New Seeds of Contemplation

FEELINGS, feely-feely feelings. We hear so much about feelings. It's the triumph of the therapeutic. The self-help gurus proclaim the gospel of getting in touch with your feelings. Thus do they rake in the dough, the bucks, the greenbacks, the moolah. Thus do they rake it in. But genuine spiritual guides, to a one, over the centuries, caution us to take our feelings with a grain of salt. Feelings can be misleading.

Take an Advent memo. Love is not a feeling, not the kind of love that stands the test of time. Love, the spiritually wise tell us, is at rock bottom an act of the will. St. Thomas Aquinas taught in the 13th century that love is an act of the will. Plain as the nose on your face. An act of the will. Not a feeling. This does not mean we should scorn loosey-goosey feelings of romantic love. Enjoy them, but don't expect loosey-goosey to carry you over the long haul. Hardly.

Take an Advent memo. Joy also is deeper than feelings. You can find joy in the Nazi death camps of World War II, and today you can find joy in people who take care of people who have the most terrible diseases. Joy, true joy, is not superficial. Give slick preachers of sunshine a wide berth, Merton advised. For their message has no depth.

When prayer brings loosey-goosey feelings of comfort and joy, enjoy the fizz while it lasts but don't expect it to last. Live on a deeper level than that. That's the ticket.

God of quiet Advent joy, help me to welcome emotional and spiritual comfort when it comes, but help me to cultivate love and joy regardless of how I feel. Amen.

Third Sunday of Advent

"[God] says, "Do not blame yourself too much, thinking that your trouble and distress is all your fault. For it is not my will that you should be unduly sad and despondent."

— JULIAN OF NORWICH, Revelations of Divine Love

YOU GOT TROUBLE AND DISTRESS, I got trouble and distress, all God's children got trouble and distress. So don't feel like the Lone Ranger. Thing is, it is not God's will that we should feel bummed out all the time. Someone said, "A sad Christian is a *sad Christian.* "

Why do we think that if we have "trouble and distress" it must be all our fault? Why are we so inclined to beat up on ourselves for the slightest reason? Advent is the season of hope and expectation, hope and quiet joy. Yet because Advent happens the same time as the Great Shopping Binge, we sometimes feel down, even depressed, if we can't buy many expensive gifts for all kinds of people.

This is understandable. It's a cultural thing, and we can't separate ourselves from our culture, even if it is materialism run rampant. That's the way it goes. What we can do is steep ourselves more in Advent as an antidote to the spirit of the Great Shopping Binge. We can expose ourselves more to the quiet spirit of Advent thus becoming less disturbed by any sadness or distress we may experience due to a financial inability to go on an unrestrained Shopping Binge for those we love.

Advent is the time to look forward to the blessings of love, forgiveness, and reconciliation that result from the coming of the Son of God and son of Mary into the world. This is what the weeks before Christmas are about. The more we focus on this, the less power the Great Shopping Binge will have over us. And the more joy we will know when Christmas does arrive.

Lord of Advent, I know you do not want me
to be too sad about anything. Help me to turn
my troubles and distresses over to you. Amen.

Third Monday of Advent

"Radio is a machine producing absolute verbal noise. The content hardly matters any longer; the production of noise is the main concern. It is as though words were being ground down by radio, transformed into an amorphous mass."

— Max Picard, The World of Silence

LISTEN. Do you want to know a secret? *Doo-dah-doo.* Closer. Let me whisper in your ear. Here it is. Advent is a quiet season, but everywhere we go we are surrounded by noises, music, words flying through the air, pummeling our ears constantly. Often, we become dependent on the noises, music, and words produced by electronic devices. We get jumpy and nervous if we don't have them. We get so we can't cope with quiet. Put the average person in a quiet room and after fifteen minutes he or she will become nervous and agitated. Some folks can't drive around in a car without turning on the radio. Others can't fall asleep at night unless they have a radio or recorded music playing nearby.

We don't listen to the words, music, noises that fly at us all the time from radio, television sets turned on but not watched, "background music" in stores, elevators, shopping malls. We don't listen to the words, music, and miscellaneous noises produced by a noisy world. They are simply there driving away the quiet.

But Advent is a quiet season, a quiet season of waiting patiently in expectation of a Wondrous Event. But how can wonder grow if there is no quiet? The shepherds waited quietly in the fields. The magi traveled quietly. Joseph and Mary waited quietly, as did the animals in the stable. Where can we find some quiet in our Advent?

Lord of Advent, help me to cultivate a quiet heart so you may be born there anew on Christmas. Amen.

Third Tuesday of Advent

*"There are people who cannot keep the first commandment because in their heart of hearts they are afraid to keep the second. They look upon human love as something which competes with the love of God, not as it is — something which completes it.... This in spite of the words of Christ, who said that it is **impossible** to love God and not to love one another, and who implored His followers with His dying breath to love one another."*

— CARYLL HOUSELANDER, The Reed of God

ADVENT IS NOT completely overwhelmed by the Great Shopping Binge. Not completely. In most cities and towns we also hear about activities geared to nothing more than giving to those who have less. Food banks. Toys for Tots. Winter coat collections for children. Soup kitchens. Salvation Army bell ringers stand in front of stores where the Great Shopping Binge is going on. Local organizations of various kinds take up collections to buy and distribute food and clothing at Christmas. The message of giving for its own sake and unselfishness as an end in itself peeks through here and there, now and then.

Indeed, the tradition of gift-giving at Christmas originated with the idea that since God gives so much to us we should give gifts to one another. We give to one another and in so doing we give to God. Well might we remember the same all during the year. Our love for God only becomes real when we show active love for other people. Indeed, the experience of God's love naturally compels us to love our neighbors.

Other people are not a distraction from the spiritual life. Other people are central to the spiritual life. Indeed, Christ would not have come into the world were this not so. God's love and human love are a package deal. That's one of the messages of Advent.

Loving God of Advent, help me to see you present in the people in my life, and help me to love them by serving them. Amen.

Third Wednesday of Advent

"You have given your holy body to strengthen my weak mind and body, and you have given your word for a lamp to my feet. Without these two things I cannot live as I ought, for the word of God is the light of my soul, and your Sacrament the bread that gives me life."

— Thomas à Kempis, The Imitation of Christ

ADVENT IS A TIME of quiet hope and expectation. But it is also a time to recall that we cannot live as we ought as long as we simply "go with the flow." The secular world bombards us daily with secular values, beliefs and assumptions that know nothing of God's love or a spiritual life. Advent is a special time that reminds us that our values, beliefs and assumptions are different. We look forward to Christmas for reasons many people know nothing about or to which they only give lip service.

How can we keep our faith alive if we don't nourish it? Have we forgotten the importance of frequent participation in the Eucharist? Have we ever taken seriously the need to pray daily with the scriptures? These two sources of spiritual nourishment never go out of style. In fact, we can't live as we ought without them. We can't.

Advent is the season of hope and expectation, but do we give this hope and expectation more than token allegiance? Do this hope and this expectation stir us deeply, touch our heart? Does this hope hit us where we live? Does this expectation mean anything to us? Can we go to the trouble to get to Mass more than once a week during Advent? Can we take the trouble to spend a few minutes each day with scripture?

If we do these things, Advent will come alive in unexpected ways. Truly unexpected ways.

Loving Lord, help me to make extra efforts
to nourish my loving intimacy with you. Amen.

Third Thursday of Advent

"The time of action does not differ from that of prayer. I possess God as peacefully in the bustle of my kitchen, where sometimes several people are asking me for different things at the same time, as I do upon my knees before the Holy Sacrament."

— BROTHER LAWRENCE,
The Practice of the Presence of God

A BRIEF MEDITATION upon Advent leads us to ask a question: Where do we find God? In the months prior to the birth of the Christ child, what did Mary do? According to the Gospel of Luke, Mary does not sit around contemplating the mystery of what is happening to her. Instead, she dashes off to visit her cousin Elizabeth for three months. No doubt she helped Elizabeth prepare for the birth of her own child.

We think of Advent as a season of hope and a season of expectation. But perhaps Advent should also be a season of service. Perhaps we will find Christ in Christmas on a deeper level if during Advent we take on a special form of service to others with special needs.

What can we do, first of all, for the other members of our family or the other people we live or work with? What special needs do they have for acceptance, understanding, forgiveness and love? We concern ourselves with buying gifts, but do we try to think of new ways to share our very selves?

We tend to think of Advent as a "churchy" season, something we think about on Sundays in church. But Advent has far more meaning on Sundays if it is real for us the other six days of the week. Advent is an everyday holy season, an everyday opportunity to prepare for the coming of Christ at Christmas by showing special care for others.

Lord of Advent, stir my heart to awareness of your presence in the activities of my everyday life. Amen.

Third Friday of Advent

"If we are not humble, we tend to demand that faith must also bring with it good health, peace of mind, good luck, success in business, popularity, world peace, and every other good thing we can imagine. And it is true that God can give us all these good things if He wants to. But they are of no importance compared with faith, which is essential. If we insist on other things as the price of our believing, we tend by that very fact to undermine our own belief. I do not think it would be an act of mercy on God's part simply to let us get away with this!"

— Thomas Merton, New Seeds of Contemplation

THE MESSAGES AND MEANINGS of Advent are many. Advent, oh Advent, what do you have to say to us? Come. Hold our hand and tell us what you have to say. Advent puts an arm around our shoulder. Advent confides in us: See. My messages are many but they are simple. Listen. God's love comes with no strings attached. No strings. No red tape. No bureaucratic mumbo-jumbo. Strings, tape, mumbo-jumbo, all these echo sinfulness and of these God knows nothing. Nothing.

God's love comes with no strings attached, Advent says again. Where the strings come from, the red tape, the mumbo-jumbo, is from your side of the relationship, your side of the faith relationship you have with God. God offers everything and asks for everything in return, but you say maybe this, or if that. Then I will give everything in return. Good health, more than enough money and material comfort, good luck, peace of mind — give me all these and then I will believe, then I will give everything in return.

Advent speaks: My message, year after year, time after time, is that God gives everything, no strings attached, even if you do not respond by giving everything in return. God still gives everything, and that's the message of Christmas Day.

*Lord Jesus, help me to put no conditions
on my love for you and my love for those
I live and work with. Amen.*

Third Saturday of Advent

"As truly as God is our father, so just as truly is he our mother. In our father, God Almighty, we have our being; in our merciful mother we are remade and restored. Our fragmented lives are knit together and made perfect man. And by giving and yielding ourselves, through grace, to the Holy Spirit we are made whole."

— JULIAN OF NORWICH, Revelations of Divine Love

ONE OF THE IMAGES of Advent: the Christmas manger scene in the church or in our home, all the figures arranged, Mary here, Joseph there, the shepherds thus, the animals just so, maybe the magi over there. But during Advent, the season of patient waiting, the crib is empty, waiting, ready to be the resting place of the Child.

What does this image of Advent teach us? Mary here, Joseph there. In the waiting love of Mary and Joseph we may see God's love in a special way, an Advent way. Mary and Joseph are mother and father, awaiting the birth of the Child. Mary and Joseph together reflect God's motherly and fatherly love as it exists for each of us, waiting, waiting for each of us to come to birth in our heart and in our soul. Waiting in love.

During Advent we wait and look forward to the birth of the Child. But during Advent God also waits. God waits for us and perhaps God wonders. Will we draw closer this year? God is closer to us than we are to ourselves, but how close are we to realizing this and living as if it's true? Oh, remarkable. We have an Advent God, a waiting God, a God constantly looking out the window awaiting our return. Imagine that.

*God of Advent, help me to draw closer to you
as you have drawn closer to me. Amen.*

Fourth Sunday of Advent

"In winter silence is visible: the snow is silence become visible.

"The space between heaven and earth is occupied by silence; heaven and earth are merely the edge of the snowy silence.

"Snowflakes meet in the air and fall together on to the earth, which is already white in the silence. Silence meeting silence.

"People stand silent on the side of the street. Human language is covered by the snow of silence. What remains of man is his body standing in the snow like a milestone of silence. People stand still and silence moves between them."

— MAX PICARD, The World of Silence

D O YOU LIVE in a snowy land? Or do you remember living in a snowy land at an earlier time in your life, waking up to find the world under snow? The first snowfall of the winter. Remember. Look out a window at the first snowfall of the year and capture the silence in your heart. Everything is quiet; the snow muffles sound. In the snow, under the fall of snow, the world becomes an Advent place, waiting quietly, waiting for whatever destiny the snow may bring. Waiting quietly.

Sing a song of Advent, pocket full of sky. Four and twenty snow birds all begin to fly. There are no words, there is no poetry wide enough to hold the mystery that is Advent. As we step into the last week of Advent we realize, with chagrin, that Advent is always beginning. Even as Advent starts the slow, quiet walk toward its own end we know that it never ends. Even on Christmas, we know that life itself is one long Advent, waiting, looking forward, moving toward the beginning that is the end of life. Life is one long Advent moving toward the Christmas that is our ultimate destiny. Each Advent reminds us of this. Each Advent reminds us.

Loving God of Advent, help me to cherish the spirit of Advent all through the year. Amen.

Fourth Monday of Advent

"Advent is the season of the secret, the secret of the growth of Christ, of Divine Love growing in silence.

"It is the season of humility, silence, and growth.

"For nine months Christ grew in His Mother's body. By His own will she formed Him from herself, from the simplicity of her daily life."

— CARYLL HOUSELANDER, The Reed of God

THAT'S IT, of course. Advent holds a secret, a secret we uncover only on Christmas. We uncover the secret, but it doesn't stop being a secret. It's the secret of the coming into the world of the Son of God. It doesn't stop being a secret. If anything, it only becomes a bigger secret than it was before. Imagine that.

During Advent we, like Mary, are called to let Christ grow in us from the simplicity of our daily life. We are called to allow Christ to form himself in us. From the inside out. This is the special message of Advent, and this is the purpose of the Christian life. Baptism sows the seeds of Christ in us, and we are to cultivate them and allow them to grow and bear fruit. Imagine that.

We look forward to the birth of Christ, soon and very soon, at Christmas. But this is not just an event "out there." Advent reminds us, day by day, that Christ is born in the silence of our own heart. On Christmas we remind ourselves that Christ is born in us. This is where it matters for Christ to be born. If Christ is not born in us then Christmas is little more than tinsel and bright lights. But if we allow Christ to be born in us, if we invite him to be born in us, if we open wide the doors of our soul and let him be born in us, then Christmas is all it is meant to be.

Lord Jesus, help me to open my heart to you and allow you to be born in me this Christmas. Amen.

Fourth Tuesday of Advent

"Do not take it to heart if you see others honored and distinguished, while you are passed over and left in obscurity. Lift up your heart to me in heaven, and you will not be hurt by the contempt of people on earth."

— Thomas à Kempis, The Imitation of Christ

ADVENT LIFE, we are well and truly steeped in Advent life. On the verge of Christmas now. Advent hope charges the air like electricity. We hold our breath with anticipation. O come, O come, Emmanuel. Silently waits the world for the coming of . . . what?

What do we wait for? We wait for Christmas. But who comes at Christmas? Jesus. And who is Jesus, who was Jesus? We pray for the coming of Jesus at Christmas, but do we know what we're praying for? When was the last time we thought about it? When was the last time we picked up the Gospels to see what Jesus says and what Jesus does? Jesus is born, he lives, teaches and heals. Then he dies a horrible death. He is one of the great failures of all history. For this we wait?

Of course, there is the Resurrection. But what does this mean? "Resurrection" is a word we use to talk about a huge mystery of faith. It's a word we use to talk about something we can't begin to understand. We know "Resurrection" means eternal life, victory over death, but that's about all we know. It definitely does not mean escape from death. We still must die. Jesus still had to die a terrible death. So at Christmas we await the birth of a Child who fails big-time, prior to his victory. That we do not understand.

During Advent we can keep in mind that the glories and honors of this world have little meaning. In fact, they don't give out honors and awards for doing what matters most in this life. They don't give out awards for living with faith, hope, and love.

God of Advent, help me to care more about being the kind of person you want me to be than the kind of person the world wants me to be. Amen.

Fourth Wednesday of Advent

"One must serve God in a holy liberty and do one's work faithfully without distress or anxiety, calling the soul gently and quietly back to God so soon as we find it drawn away from him. It is, however, needful to put all one's confidence in God and unburden oneself of all other cares, even of many personal devotions which, very good though they may be, we inadvisedly take upon ourselves."

— BROTHER LAWRENCE,
The Practice of the Presence of God

ADVENT IS A QUIET SEASON, a season of hope and a season of expectation, of looking forward to the coming of the Messiah. But listen. Advent is also a time to appreciate more deeply the ongoing presence of the Holy Spirit in our midst. Look. The Holy Spirit whispers blessings, day in, day out. The Holy Spirit prays in our heart constantly, "with sighs too deep for words" (Rom 8:26).

Whispers and sighs, whispers and sighs. Blessings and prayers, blessings and prayers. We live constantly caressed by the Holy Spirit's whispered blessings and prayerful sighs. No matter what may be happening on the surface of our life, the deeper reality is whispered blessings and prayerful sighs. See. This is why distress and anxiety are useless. Whatever sparks distress and anxiety is real, make no mistake about that. But it is also passing. This, too, shall pass.

In the long run, on a much deeper level, in a much more real way, the truth is whispered blessings and prayerful sighs. Whispers and sighs, blessings and prayers. We can sink beneath our distress and anxiety to where there are whispered blessings and prayerful sighs. We can. And when we do, then we are in communion with the true spirit of Advent. Then we are.

Lord Jesus, Messiah, help me to give less attention to the distress and anxiety in my life and more attention to the blessings and prayers. Amen.

Fourth Thursday of Advent

"God's love is like a river springing up in the depth of the Divine Substance and flowing endlessly through His creation, filling all things with life and goodness and strength."

— THOMAS MERTON, New Seeds of Contemplation

HERE IS THE TRUTH of Advent, here is the truth of Advent as it gives birth, with joy, to Christmas. Here is the truth. See: God was and is so in love with all of creation that Jesus became a part of that creation. The Son of God became fully human, fully a creature, while retaining the fullness of divinity. Oh, here. Oh, there. God is everywhere. God is everywhere not only reflected in creation but creation is profoundly holy because the Son of God became a part of it, took it to himself and so blessed it in its essence.

This is what it's about, you know. You know. Advent leads us into the truth that all of creation is filled "with life and goodness and strength." Oh, here. Oh, there. Oh, everywhere. There is no place you can go that you will not find life and goodness and strength. Even in the face of tragedy, pain and anguish, through it and on the other side you will find life and goodness and strength, even more than you found before. Even more.

God's love has no limits, knows no boundaries. God wanted to be everywhere and in everything, even creation itself, even human nature — especially human nature, but God did not become a tree, a rock, a river or one of his glorious creatures in the animal kingdom. God became a human being. So God's love is everywhere, but in a special and profound way God's love is in people, in ourselves and in others. God's love is in people. This is the truth of Advent as it gives birth to Christmas. Oh, here. Oh, there. Oh, everywhere.

God of Advent joy, help me to be more sensitive
to your love present everywhere, especially
in myself and in other people. Amen.

Fourth Friday of Advent

"Our faith is a light, the kindly gift of that endless day which is our Father, God. By this light our Mother Christ, and our good Lord the Holy Spirit lead us in this fleeting life. [God says:] "I love you, and you love me, and our love shall never be broken."

— JULIAN OF NORWICH, Revelations of Divine Love

METAPHORS for the Divine Mystery flying through the air every which way. Up, down, and around, and the ones that startle us the most have special value. The old standbys, like "Father" and "Lord" are soft as a feather bed. Can't do without them. But the metaphors that startle us help us to recall that we can't put God in a box. They help us see our God in new ways and from new perspectives. In a new light.

During Advent we recall that when the Son of God came into the world as a tiny baby, this is something completely new, unexpected, and unpredictable — and to some, unacceptable. What? God as a human infant? Absurd! Yet this is what we believe, the most startling idea of all. We grow used to the idea, however, and it becomes soft as a feather bed, no longer shocking. So new metaphors can help awaken in us once again our amazement at a God we never can pin down.

God is an "endless day," and in the light of this "day" we see "our Mother Christ" and "our good Lord the Holy Spirit." The message: that God loves us, and we love God, and this love "shall never be broken." Metaphors, new and startling, flying through the air. Fresh as a splash of cold spring water in the face, waking us up to the eternally new God.

And the message, now and always, is love.

Loving God, help me to appreciate more deeply
all kinds of startling metaphors for you
and for your love which knows no limits. Amen.

Christmas Eve

"Marriage, which seems to us to be such a wonderful consummation of love, is only a faint shadow, a kind of symbol, of the wedding of the Spirit of God to humanity; and it is from that wedding that Christ is born into the world."

— CARYLL HOUSELANDER, The Reed of God

CHRISTMAS EVE, the day before the deep and holy Feast of the Incarnation. The day before. Can it be? Is Advent over already? "Time went by so quickly," wrote singer/song writer John Stewart, "that I didn't see it go. / But I never saw it coming so how was I to know?"

That's life, and that's Advent. Over so quickly.

Time, sacred time. Weeks gone so soon, and now we verge on Christmas. It's such a great mystery that we find ourselves stammering in the face of the goodness and silence and joy of it all. We find ourselves reaching out to claim, once again, the spirit of childhood. This is what we do on Christmas Eve. We long to know for at least a moment the spirit of childhood which is the true spirit of Christmas. Dear God, let me be a child again on Christmas Eve, if only for a moment.

We wait, we wait. We pray. We breathe deeply and wait, hoping for the grace of Christmas to bring us the whistling, wondering, bright-eyed spirit of childhood. We pray for this gift because we long to be like Christ in every way, even in his childhood. To receive Christmas in our heart we need to regain on Christmas Eve, if only for an instant, the spirit of the childhood of Christ.

Let it be, then. Let us pray to receive the spirit of childhood on Christmas Eve, if only for an instant, so we may be ready to receive the Christ Child in our heart. Let it be. Let it be.

Lord Jesus, Son of God and son of Mary, give me the spirit of childhood on this Christmas Eve that I might know the true spirit of Christmas. Amen.

Christmas

"As a magnifying glass concentrates the rays of the sun into a little burning knot of heat that can set fire to a dry leaf or a piece of paper, so the mystery of Christ in the Gospel concentrates the rays of God's light and fire to a point that sets fire to the spirit of man. And this is why Christ was born and lived in the world and died and returned from death and ascended to His Father in heaven. . . . "

— THOMAS MERTON, New Seeds of Contemplation

I MAGINE that you are sleeping by a river. Imagine that you are sleeping by a river in a forest. You are lying on your back, and you open your eyes. The cloudless, warm summer night sky is filled with countless twinkling stars, and you are alone. The sound of the wide river splashing over large boulders is almost musical, it fills you with quiet delight. There are many fish in the river, like aquatic angels, swimming deep in the current, swimming silently, beautifully powerful rainbow trout of various sizes. Near the surface, the starlight glistens on their scales. You think of the fish deep in the river, swimming and at rest. Like aquatic angels.

Listen, oh Advent pilgrim, today you reach your destination and your pilgrimage continues. This is the truth of Christmas. This is the truth. Because Christ came into the world, became one of us, we are like the stars in the night sky, shining now with a clarity that is God's own life in us. God's own life in us. Imagine that. We are submerged in the Divine Mystery of Love that is our source of vitality like the river in which the beautiful, strong rainbow trout-angels swim and rest. God is the depth in which we live and move and have our being. All because of Christmas. This is the truth of Christmas. This is the truth, pure, simple, and glorious.

"Angels we have heard on high . . . / *Gloria in excelsis Deo*."

Lord Jesus, born this day in Bethlehem and in our hearts, bless us with all the joy of this day of days. Amen and again Amen.

Editions of the Spiritual Classics Quoted in This Book

The Reed of God, by Caryll Houselander. Christian Classics, Inc., 1985.

The World of Silence, by Max Picard. Regnery/Gateway, Inc., 1952.

New Seeds of Contemplation, by Thomas Merton. New Directions, 1961.

The Imitation of Christ, by Thomas à Kempis. Translated by Betty I. Knott. Collins/Fontana Books, 1963.

Enfolded in Love: Daily Readings with Julian of Norwich (Selections from *Revelations of Divine Love*). The Seabury Press, 1980.

The Practice of the Presence of God, by Brother Lawrence. Translated by E. M. Blaiklock. Thomas Nelson Publishers, 1981.